CONTENTS

BODY IN ACTION

HEALTH AND FITNESS

HEALTH AND FITNESS

Healthy Eating

A Healthy Diet

Eating the right things

Where animals live depends on the type of food they eat. They can only survive in places where there is plenty of the particular sort of food they need. Human beings, on the other hand, have successfully adapted themselves to many kinds of food, so they have been able to settle in even the most hostile places on Earth.

We can make the most of the food available to us and, more importantly, we can use our intelligence to choose the types of food that are good for us.

During the history of human development, we have learnt which foods are good for us. Today we also know exactly how much to eat and what kind of food we need to be healthy and avoid modern-day health hazards.

There's a saying: "Eat to live don't live to eat" which means you should eat just enough of the right things for healthy living. Don't let your liking for food which is not good for you rule your eating habits. Don't eat too much either!

Living to eat, or eating to live?

People around the world have different eating habits. We all eat the same sorts of food, containing the nutrients the body needs, but they are cooked in different ways. In some developing countries, there is so little to eat that many people die of starvation and malnutrition. In the West, on the other hand, health problems are caused by over-eating certain types of food.

We all know that food is vital for us to stay alive. If you do not eat, you get an unpleasant feeling in the stomach and sometimes hunger can even make you bad-tempered. Through a series of complicated mechanisms, your brain tells you that you need new energy. If you do not eat your blood sugar level goes down. In order to nourish themselves, the cells have to fall back on energy reserves. The contractions of the stomach become stronger and you begin to be aware of the feeling of hunger.

These are signs that your body needs fuel to function. You must use your intelligence to choose the right food which will provide your body with the necessary balance of nutrients.

It's never too early to start eating a sensible diet! A badly-balanced diet in childhood can damage you for the rest of your life and lead to all kinds of problems which are connected with bad eating habits, such as obesity, diabetes, tooth decay, vitamin deficiency and so on. So be careful! Always see food as a special substance which is essential to life and learn to enjoy eating food that is good for you.

What is food made of?

Every second, 50 million cells die off in your body and they have to be replaced by the same number of new cells. As well as energy, your body must also have the substances needed to make these 50 million cells per second. These substances are contained in the food you eat. There are three main groups of food:

● **Restorative foods** are the proteins which form living matter.

● **Invigorating foods** provide the energy needed for the various parts of the body to function (breathing, heartbeat, maintaining the body temperature and so on). Fats and carbohydrates belong to this group.

● **Regulating foods** affect the chemical reactions that control the workings of our organs and tissues. Water, vitamins and minerals (including sodium, calcium, phosphorus, iron, magnesium and iodine) belong to this group.

Proteins, the building blocks of life

The foods which are highest in protein are meat, fish, pulses (beans and lentils), milk and eggs. Proteins are transformed into amino acids by the chemical action of digestive juices. Foods containing protein are very important because proteins build up your body, helping you grow and making sure that your body tissues are renewed.

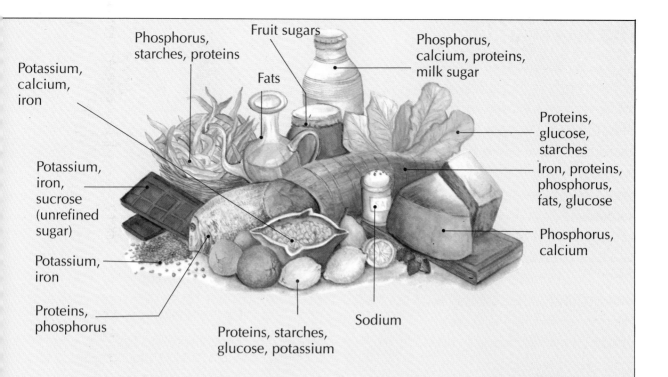

Potassium, calcium, iron

Phosphorus, starches, proteins

Fruit sugars

Fats

Phosphorus, calcium, proteins, milk sugar

Proteins, glucose, starches

Iron, proteins, phosphorus, fats, glucose

Phosphorus, calcium

Potassium, iron, sucrose (unrefined sugar)

Potassium, iron

Proteins, phosphorus

Proteins, starches, glucose, potassium

Sodium

Sugars, a source of energy

Fruit, cereals such as wheat and barley, bread, potatoes and honey are very rich in sugars. Sugars and starch are both **carbohydrates**. In the digestive process they are converted into simpler types of sugars – the simplest form is grape sugar, or **glucose**, which the body can use immediately. Glucose is the body's main source of fuel.

Fats are energy reserves

Foods which contain fats are very high in energy. When there is no glucose available the body uses fats as fuel. Fats are found in vegetable oils, margarine, milk, butter, eggs, dried fruit and meat.

Vitamins and minerals

If you want to avoid serious illnesses, you must make sure that there are enough vitamins in the food you eat. The body cannot produce vitamins itself so it has to take up vitamins through the food you eat. Most vitamins are found in plants and dairy products. Vitamins have been named after certain letters of the alphabet (A, B, C, D, E and K).

Your body cannot produce minerals either. If you do not take large enough amounts of minerals through your food, your health could be seriously damaged.

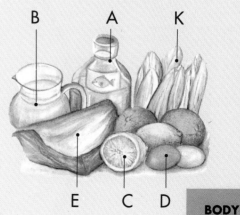

B   A   K

E   C   D

The water of life

As you already know, nearly 75 per cent of your body is made up of water. You could survive a month or more without food, but without liquid you could only survive two or three days at the most. If you lose 20 per cent of the water in your body you could die of dehydration.

The feeling of thirst is the alarm signal sent by the brain to tell you that you must drink. If your body does not contain enough fluid, urine cannot be produced. This means that the poisonous substances which have collected in the blood cannot be flushed out, and they may poison the tissues. Drinking is absolutely vital for your body. It is the only way to make up for your body's constant loss of fluid. If you lose more fluid than you take in, you could have serious health problems.

STONE AGE MENU

Our prehistoric ancestors chose their food for its colour, taste and availability. They learnt which foods were edible and which were poisonous – something they were certainly only able to do after some unfortunate experiences.

Two of the most important events that affected people's eating habits were the use of fire, which allowed indigestible food to be made edible by cooking, and the invention of pottery to cook in. Eating habits also began to change as people started growing, or cultivating, food. Then they gradually moved from a diet based mainly on meat to a diet of carbohydrates (especially cereals).

In the course of time our ancestors learnt about the goodness and taste of various foods, and were able to reject foods which were unsuitable to eat.

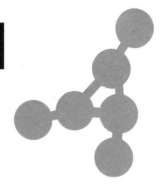

Types Of Food

Cereals – a basic food

Cereals are grains used as food. They are important because of the high energy content. They are rich in vitamin B and their husks (coverings, which are also known as bran) have a high fibre content.

The inner part of the cereal grain is very rich in carbohydrate (a starch) and proteins, while the germ (the shoot from which the grain grows) contains valuable vegetable fats and vitamin E.

Ever since humans first started to cultivate cereals, we have never stopped finding new ways of using them. Cereals are the basis of many foods and they form the most important part of our daily diet. Just think of the many dishes which can be prepared with rice, wheat, maize, barley or rye, not forgetting bread of course! According to nutritional scientists, cereals should make up two-thirds of our diet.

Flour

Bread dough

Wheat

Bread

From cereal grains to bread

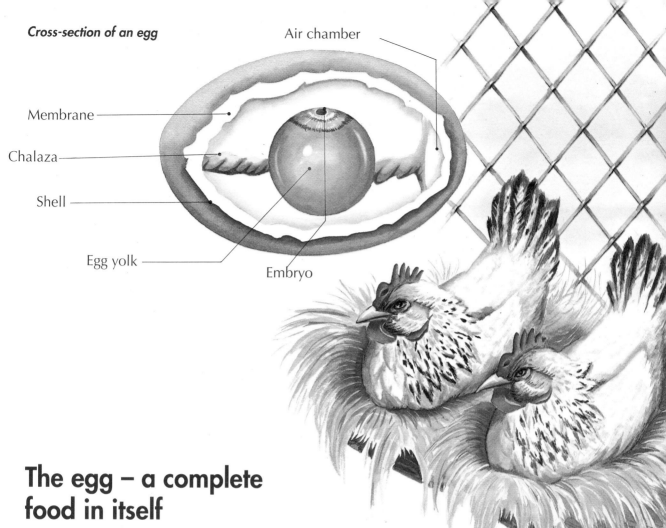

Cross-section of an egg

Air chamber

Membrane

Chalaza

Shell

Egg yolk

Embryo

The egg – a complete food in itself

The egg is a perfect food because it contains many nutrients, which are needed for the embryo to develop. A large chicken's egg weighs about 60 grams and it is made up of the following things:

● **20 grams of yolk**, containing high levels of fats, proteins, iron and other minerals, as well as vitamins A, B, D and E.

● **30 grams of egg white**, containing a large amount of water as well as a protein called albumen.

● **10 grams of shell and membrane**.

Remarkably, the egg is a complete food which has been entirely produced by nature, with its own natural packaging. It keeps for a long time and

Most of the eggs we eat come from chickens. What good friends they are, producing a complete food, neatly packaged.

it can be prepared in many different ways. The only disadvantage of the egg is that it contains a lot of cholesterol – people who suffer from heart and circulation problems should therefore not eat too many eggs.

How much energy do you need?

The energy which you get from the various foods you eat is measured in **calories**. The number of calories you need depends on the amount of energy you use. Therefore if the food you eat contains more calories than you use, you will put on weight. Some people burn up calories more quickly than others, so they can eat more without having to worry about putting

The body uses energy constantly, even when you are resting. When you are taking part in physical activities or in sport, you burn up more calories than when you are studying or watching TV.

Playing

Studying

on weight. Any energy which has not been used is turned into fat and stored in the body.

Obesity can lead to serious health problems (especially heart-related diseases). If your body weight is 20 per cent or more over the normal weight for your height and age, you are considered obese. You should be very careful not to store up more energy than you really need. The amount and the kind of food you need depends on your age and how physically active you are. A well-balanced diet should:

● only provide as much energy as you need,

● replace the energy you have used up,

● include restorative foods such as proteins which make sure that the body cells are renewed.

An 11- or 12-year-old child needs to take in 2,000 to 2,500 calories every day.

Working

Doing sport

The importance of fish in your diet

Fish is an extremely important source of proteins, minerals (especially iodine and phosphorus) and vitamin B, and therefore it should feature regularly in your diet. The only things to watch out for are the bones!

Sea fish and freshwater fish are divided into two main groups:

● **Oily fish** (such as herring, sardines, mackerel and tuna fish) contain between 5 and 30 per cent oil. They are very high in calories – 100 to 285 per 100 grams. Oily fish are rich in iron and vitamins A, D and E.

● **White fish** (sole, cod, hake and plaice, for example) contain hardly any oil but a lot of water. They have only 50 to 100 calories per 100 grams, and they are easily digested and very nourishing.

White fish are high in vitamins and their only disadvantage is that they are highly perishable (they decay quickly). That is why white fish must be bought deep frozen or very fresh and eaten quickly.

The sea is like a full larder. For a long time now, we have been using the sea as a dumping ground, endangering its unique ecosystem, and with it an irreplaceable link in the great chain of life.

Why eat meat?

Meat, which is the muscle of animals, is a rich source of protein. The muscle is made up of muscle fibre and tissue which are both rich in proteins and fats.

People eat meat from over a hundred kinds of animals. On the whole, poultry is less fatty than beef, and beef is less fatty than lamb and pork. In general meat contains a lot of iron, potassium and phosphorus but little calcium. It is high in vitamin B but low in carbohydrates.

There are many people who do not eat meat. They are called **vegetarians**. They either do not like the taste of meat or they do not believe in eating animals. Vegetarians get their proteins from vegetables such as beans, nuts and lentils

Meat is low in carbohydrates. It is very nutritious because it is high in proteins, fats and vitamins A, B and E.

THE GOODNESS IN FOOD				
Food (100 g)	Calories	Protein (g)	Vitamins	Main minerals
MILK AND DAIRY PRODUCTS				
Cows' milk	65-69	3.5	A, D, B	Calcium, phosphorus
Mothers' milk	60-62	1.2-2.01	A, D, B	Calcium, phosphorus
Butter	675-790	0.8	A, D	Calcium, phosphorous
Parmesan cheese	325-420	27	A, D, B	Calcium, phosphorus
Yogurt	32-69	3.5	B	Calcium, phosphorus
MEAT AND FISH				
Egg	100-166	12-13	A, B, D, E	Iron, phosphorus, calcium
Beef	140-200	20	A	Calcium, phosphorus
Pork	250-300	18	B	Iron, phosphorus
Lamb	250	15	A. B	Iron, phosphorus
Poultry	150	20	A, B	Iron, phosphorus
Liver	130	20	A, B, C, D, E	Iron
Ham	340	15	B	Iron, phosphorus
Sole	147	17	B	Phosphorus
Mussels	50-80	6-15		Calcium
Tuna fish	270	28	B	Phosphorus
Sardines in oil	200-250	19	A, D, E, K	Phosphorus
Anchovies	506	18	B	Phosphorus
GRAIN				
Rice	350	4.6	B	
Wheat	350	10-13	B, E	Calcium, iron, phosphorus
Cooked spaghetti	360-380	10-14	B, E	Calcium, iron, phosphorus
FRUIT AND VEGETABLES				
Apricots	37-50	0.7-0.9	C	
Cherries	50-60	0.8-1.2	C	
Plums	48-53	0.7-0.8	C	
Strawberries	40	0.6	C	
Lemons	30-40	0.3-0.9	C	
Apples	56	0.4	C	
Peaches	42-55	0.7-0.9	C	
Melons	30	0.7	C	
Oranges	45-61	0.8-1	C	
Beans	100	6	B	
Cooked courgettes	60	0.6		
Spinach	22-38	1.5-3.3	A. B	Calcium and iron
Chickpeas	400	25	B, E	
Peas	80-90	6.4-6.7	B	
Green beans	39-50	2.4-5	B	Potassium
Lettuce	10-15	1-1.3	A, B, C	
Potato chips	340	4	C	Potassium
Raw tomatoes	20-22	0.9-1.0	A, C	

Vegetables are good for you

It is impossible to say how many kinds of vegetables there are in the world. There are green vegetables such as spinach, and types with bulbs such as onions and garlic. Then there are root vegetables such as carrots and radishes, fruit vegetables such as aubergines, courgettes and cucumbers, stem vegetables such as celery and leeks, and flower vegetables such as artichokes and cauliflower. They all have a high nutritional value.

● Most vegetables contain between 70 and 95 per cent water.

● They prevent constipation because the fibres act as bulk material which stimulates the bowels and helps the digestion.

● Vegetables such as tomatoes and carrots contain **carotene**, which is turned into vitamin A in the body.

● Some vegetables contain vitamin C and folic acid.

● Vegetables provide nutrients which are not available in other types of food.

Cauliflower
(flower vegetable)

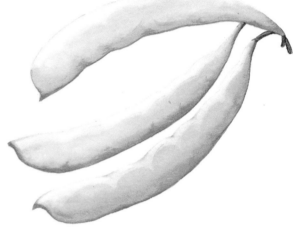

Green beans
(seed vegetable)

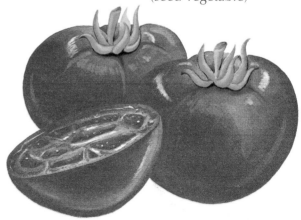

Tomatoes
(fruit vegetable)

Brightly coloured vegetables such as carrots and tomatoes, along with green vegetables, contain large amounts of carotene, which is converted into vitamin A in the body.

Fruit – healthy and delicious

Fruit is refreshing, juicy and very tasty – in short, it's a delight to eat! The sweetness of a fruit depends on its sugar content. Its refreshing quality is the result of the large amount of water it contains (the watermelon contains 90 per cent water) and its slight acidity.

Most fruits are rich in vitamin C. Oranges and lemons are a famous source of vitamin C, although other fruits such as blackcurrants actually contain even more vitamin C. Fresh, uncooked fruit is a rich source of vitamins. (Vitamins in foods are often largely destroyed by cooking.)

Many delicious fruits come from tropical countries but there are also excellent fruits in Europe. The Mediterranean region is famous for its citrus fruit while central and northern Europe mainly grow apples, pears, cherries and plums.

Dairy products

Milk and dairy products

Milk is our first food. A baby can survive entirely on its mother's milk from the moment of birth to the age of two without suffering from any vitamin deficiency. Milk from mammals, especially cows' milk, is an important source of nourishment for both adults and children.

Today milk can be preserved for long periods by modern techniques – pasteurisation, sterilisation and packaging. There are many products made from it:

● **Yogurt** is fermented milk. All the proteins, fats, vitamins and calcium of the milk are preserved.

● **Cream** can be taken from the top of the milk once it has been left to stand for a while after milking. Today this is done by a machine.

● **Cheese** is made from warmed milk to which rennet is added. Rennet comes from the lining of calves' stomachs, but sometimes a vegetable-based substance is used instead. The rennet makes the

Human beings have been making cheese for over 7,000 years. Many of today's popular cheeses, such as Cheddar, Roquefort and Edam, were already known in the Middle Ages. There are many types of cheeses. You may have tasted Emmental, Red Leicester, Camembert, Stilton or Parmesan. You may have also had sheep or goats' cheese or Mozzarella cheese made from buffalo milk.

milk separate into curds, which is the solid part, and whey, the watery part. The curds are thoroughly drained and become cheese.

Before the invention of the refrigerator and the discovery of pasteurisation, making cheese was the only way of keeping milk for any length of time. Cheese is very nourishing. It contains 25-35 per cent protein, calcium, vitamin A and vitamin B2 (riboflavin).

● **Butter** is concentrated milk fat (cream). The cream is beaten until it turns into solid lumps of fat, after which the remaining liquid (buttermilk) is pressed out. Butter contains a lot of vitamin A and D but no protein or calcium.

Some central and north European countries have been known as 'milk civilisations' because milk and dairy products play a very important part in the diet of the people who live there. All mountainous regions and lowland hillside areas in central and northern Europe have a tradition of dairy farming.

What is your favourite drink?

Water is the perfect drink, but you may prefer other types of drinks such as fruit juice, fizzy drinks such as cola or lemonade, tea or coffee. Adults may like wine, beer, whisky or liqueurs.

All types of drinks contain a high percentage of water:

Fruit juices are 89 per cent water.

Wine is 75 per cent water.

Beer is 92 per cent water.

Tea is 96 per cent water.

Many drinks contain other substances that may surprise you:

Coffee, **tea** and **cola** all contain **caffeine**, a stimulant which increases the activity of the brain and speeds up the rhythm of the heart. If you drink too much coffee, tea or cola, they can cause palpitations (feeling of having a harder and faster than usual heartbeat), shaking and even a feeling of being very fed up.

Beer is a low-alcohol drink made from barley. It has a high malt content – (malt is a sugar which can make you put on weight).

Wine goes perfectly with food. It is an alcoholic drink so children should not drink it, and adults should not drink too much of it.

Fruit juices are excellent when freshly squeezed. Most shop-bought juices contain flavourings, sugar and colouring. They are still good for you because they are rich in vitamin C.

Non-alcoholic drinks

Alcoholic drinks

Drinks are essential to life. However, alcoholic drinks should only be taken in small quantities because too much can be harmful to your health.

OUR DAILY BREAD

In many countries bread is the most important food. It is often made from wheat flour but sometimes rye and maize flour is also used. From a nutritional point of view, bread is not a complete food, so it must be eaten with other foods. Bread contains water, carbohydrates, proteins, fats, a few minerals and important vitamins.

For centuries bread has been more than just a basic food for many people. It has been seen as a symbol of life – in the Lord's Prayer, there is a phrase 'give us our daily bread', and there are also colloquial expressions such as 'hard-earned bread'.

The phrase 'man shall not live by bread alone' means that human beings cannot survive by just eating food to keep the body alive, but they also need an active and alert mind to be happy.

Electric oven for baking bread.

KEEPING FIT

● Swimming

The right diet gives us the energy we need to enjoy sports. Swimming is undoubtedly a sport with many advantages. For instance, you can swim at any age. Young children, and even little babies, can be taught how to swim. What are the advantages of regular swimming? It stimulates the circulation of the blood and improves the movement of oxygen to the cells. Also, when swimming, you exercise almost all the muscles in your body, so increasing their strength and resistance. Swimming is a sport where women can be just as good as men.

Swimming can play an important part in recovering from illnesses such as heart attacks. People who are recovering from an illness must swim in warm water (over 28 degrees) and the strokes must be slow and regular. There are four main swimming strokes – breast stroke, back stroke, front crawl and butterfly. The

The front crawl is the fastest stroke, but it is also possible to do the crawl at a slower speed for longer distances.

The butterfly stroke is probably the most difficult stroke. Inexperienced swimmers soon get out of breath doing this stroke.

butterfly stroke requires the greatest effort and uses up the most energy. Whatever style you choose, swimming is fun and healthy for all the family.

The art of swimming has been known since ancient times. Once you have learnt to swim you can use a whole variety of strokes to move in the water. Breast stroke is the easiest way to move in the water. It requires no strenuous movements and it is an excellent breathing exercise. It is the best style for swimming long distances.

For young people, diving from a diving board or diving platform improves the flexibility of the muscles, as well as being an excellent way of increasing control over the body. Diving is a recognised Olympic sport.

KEY WORDS

Vitamin A – found in liver, kidneys, fish-liver oils, eggs, dairy products and margarine. Needed for healthy cells, bones and teeth, and seeing in dim light.

Vitamin B – a group of vitamins including vitamins B12, B2 (riboflavin) and folic acid. Found in yeast, liver, and except B12, in wholewheat cereals and green vegetables. B2 and B12 are found in dairy products, eggs, nuts, fish, lean meat, kidneys and potatoes. Needed for healthy tissues, muscles, nerves, skin and hair. B12 and folic acid are vital for the formation of blood cells.

Vitamin C – found in green vegetables, potatoes, tomatoes and citrus fruit. Needed for healthy tissues, skin, blood vessels, bones, gums and teeth. Helps to heal wounds and fight infections.

Vitamin D – found in liver, fish-liver oils, oily fish, dairy products, egg yolk and margarine. A special substance called pro-vitamin D3 in skin cells is converted to vitamin D under sunlight. Sunlight is the best way of getting Vitamin D. Needed for absorbing calcium and phosphorus which are essential for healthy bones and teeth.

Vitamin E – found in meat, egg yolk, leafy green vegetables, nuts, dairy products, margarine, cereals, wholemeal bread, seeds and vegetable oils. Needed for cell structure and the working of enzymes. Protects lungs and other tissues from damage by pollutants. Believed to slow the ageing of cells.

Vitamin K – found in liver, fruit, nuts cereals, tomatoes, green vegetables. Essential for formation of prothrombin in liver (needed for blood clotting).

HOW MY BODY WORKS

HOW MY BODY WORKS is an educational series that builds into a complete encyclopedia of the human body. Each volume introduces and explains one of its mysteries.

In Part 33 of How My Body Works, you've found out about the types of food to eat for a healthy diet.

Part 34 takes a look at our eating habits and discovers what happens when there is a problem with the digestive system.

READ ALL ABOUT:
● **The correct way to eat**.
● **How to avoid being over-weight**.
● **What causes an upset stomach**.
● **Appendicitis** – why it is so dangerous.
● **What makes you lose your appetite**.

Albert Barillé (pictured left) is the author of this fascinating series of books. The human body is a series of complex systems and mechanisms, so to make it easier for you to understand how the body works, Barillé created The Professor, Captain Courageous, Globus, Toxicus and Virulus, plus many other colourful cartoon characters, to show you around. The Professor and his friends guide you through the body, explaining how it works in a clear and simple way that makes it fun.

TEST YOUR KNOWLEDGE
The Healthy Eating quiz

More than one answer may be correct

1. One of the main causes of health problems in the West is:
a) eating too little food
b) over-eating certain types of food
c) eating too much fruit

2. How many cells need to be replaced every second?
a) 5,000
b) 5 million
c) 50 million

3. Why do we need proteins?
a) because they help your body to grow
b) because they keep you warm in winter
c) because they make sure that your body tissues are renewed

4. What is the body's main source of fuel?
a) vitamins
b) minerals
c) glucose

5. How long can you survive without water?
a) one month
b) two weeks
c) two to three days

6. What are cereals?
a) soap operas on breakfast TV
b) grains used as food
c) the most complete food there is

7. Why is the egg a complete food?
a) because it contains many vitamins, proteins and minerals
b) because it is easy to cook
c) because it contains cholesterol

8. What is the energy you get from the foods you eat measured in?
a) litres
b) grams
c) calories

9. How many calories does an 11- or 12-year-old child need every day?
a) 2,000-2,500
b) 200-250
c) 20-25

10. Why do some people prefer not to eat meat?
a) because they do not like the idea of killing animals
b) because they do not like the taste of meat
c) because they can get the proteins they need from vegetables, nuts and pulses

ANSWERS to the '**How My Body Works**' Healthy Eating quiz are in Issue 34.
Answers to Issue 32
1 (a), 2 (c), 3 (a & b), 4 (c), 5 (b & c), 6 (b), 7 (b & c), 8 (a & c), 9 (a & b), 10 (a)

Published by
ORBIS PUBLISHING,
Griffin House,
161 Hammersmith Road,
London W6 8SD

BACK ISSUES
Back issues can be obtained by placing an order with your newsagent or, in case of difficulty, from our back numbers department. All cheques/postal orders should be made payable to Orbis Publishing Ltd.

BACK ISSUE CHARGES
Volume 1:
UK: 99p plus £1.00 p&p;
Eire: IR£0.99 plus £1.00 p&p
Thereafter:
UK: £2.99 plus 50p p&p;
Eire: IR£3.50 plus 50p p&p

ADDRESS FOR BACK ISSUES:
Orbis Publishing Ltd, Unit 10, Wheel Lane Business Park, Wheel Lane, Westfield, Hastings, East Sussex, TN35 4SG. Tel: 0424 755755

BACK ISSUES OVERSEAS
Please place requests for copies of back issues with your newsagent or, in case of difficulty, please write to the relevant address given:

Australia
Gordon and Gotch Ltd, PO Box 290, Burwood VIC 3125 (Enclose cover price plus $1 p&h per issue)

New Zealand
Gordon and Gotch (NZ) Ltd, PO Box 584, Auckland.

South Africa
Back issues Dept Republican News Agency PO Box 16034 Doornfontein 2028

Malta & Singapore
Back numbers are available at LM1.50 from your newsagent.

© Procidis Albert Barillé
© 1993 Orbis Publishing Ltd, London
N33 93 12 09
Printed in Italy
by Officine Grafiche De Agostini, Novara